Let's Read About Our Bodies

Eyes

by Cynthia Klingel and Robert B. Noyed
photographs by Gregg Andersen

Amoroso is preferred name

Reading consultant: Cecilia Minden-Cupp, Ph.D.,
Adjunct Professor, College of Continuing and Professional Studies, University of Virginia

For a free color catalog describing Weekly Reader® Early Learning Library's list of high-quality books, call 1-800-542-2595 or fax your request to (414) 332-3567.

Library of Congress Cataloging-in-Publication Data

Klingel, Cynthia.
   Eyes / by Cynthia Klingel and Robert B. Noyed.
     p. cm. — (Let's read about our bodies)
   Includes bibliographical references and index.
   Summary: A simple introduction to eyes and how they are used.
   ISBN 0-8368-3063-6 (lib. bdg.)
   ISBN 0-8368-3152-7 (softcover)
   1. Eye—Juvenile literature. [1. Eye. 2. Vision. 3. Senses and sensation.]
 I. Noyed, Robert B. II. Title.
 QP475.7.K575   2002
 612.8'4—dc21   2001054991

This edition first published in 2002 by
Weekly Reader® Early Learning Library
330 West Olive Street, Suite 100
Milwaukee, WI 53212 USA

Copyright © 2002 by Weekly Reader® Early Learning Library

An Editorial Directions book
Editors: E. Russell Primm and Emily Dolbear
Art direction, design, and page production: The Design Lab
Photographer: Gregg Andersen
Weekly Reader® Early Learning Library art direction: Tammy Gruenewald
Weekly Reader® Early Learning Library production: Susan Ashley

Printed in the United States of America

1 2 3 4 5 6 7 8 9 06 05 04 03 02

Note to Educators and Parents

As a Reading Specialist I know that books for young children should engage their interest, impart useful information, and motivate them to want to learn more.

Let's Read About Our Bodies is a new series of books designed to help children understand the value of good health and taking care of their bodies.

A young child's active mind is engaged by the carefully chosen subjects. The imaginative text works to build young vocabularies. The short, repetitive sentences help children stay focused as they develop their own relationship with reading. The bright, colorful photographs of children enjoying good health habits complement the text with their simplicity and both entertain and encourage young children to want to learn — and read — more.

These books are designed to be used by adults as "read-to" books to share with children to encourage early literacy in the home, school, and library. They are also suitable for more advanced young readers to enjoy on their own.

— Cecilia Minden-Cupp, Ph.D.,
Adjunct Professor, College of Continuing and
Professional Studies, University of Virginia

These are my eyes.
I have two eyes.

Eyes can be many colors.

I use my eyes to see. I can see big things and small things.

I use my eyes to see things that are far away.

I use my eyes to see things that are close.

Sometimes we need glasses to help us see better.

I need to keep my eyes clean and safe. I never put things in my eyes!

I wear sunglasses when it is bright outside.

My eyes work hard all day. My eyes rest at night.

Glossary

bright—filled with light

clean—free from dirt

safe—free from harm or danger

sunglasses—dark eyeglasses that protect the eyes from the Sun

For More Information

Fiction Books

Brown, Eric. *Arthur's Eyes*. Boston: Little, Brown & Co., 1983.

Seuss, Dr. *The Eye Book*. New York: Random House, 1999.

Smith, Lane. *Glasses: Who Needs 'Em?* New York: Viking, 1991.

Nonfiction Books

Ballard, Carol. *How Do Our Eyes See?* Austin, Tex.: Raintree/Steck-Vaughn, 1998.

Fowler, Allan. *How Animals See Things*. Danbury, Conn.: Children's Press, 1999.

Jedrosz, Aleksander. *Eyes*. Mahwah, N.J.: Troll, 1992.

Web Sites

A Big Look at the Eye

kidshealth.org/kid/body/eye_SW.html

For more information about the way the eye works

Index

About the Authors

Cynthia Klingel has worked as a high school English teacher and an elementary school teacher. She is currently the curriculum director for a Minnesota school district. Cynthia Klingel lives with her family in Mankato, Minnesota.

Robert B. Noyed started his career as a newspaper reporter. Since then, he has worked in school communications and public relations at the state and national level. Robert B. Noyed lives with his family in Brooklyn Center, Minnesota.